The Wandle Gu

by The Wandle Group

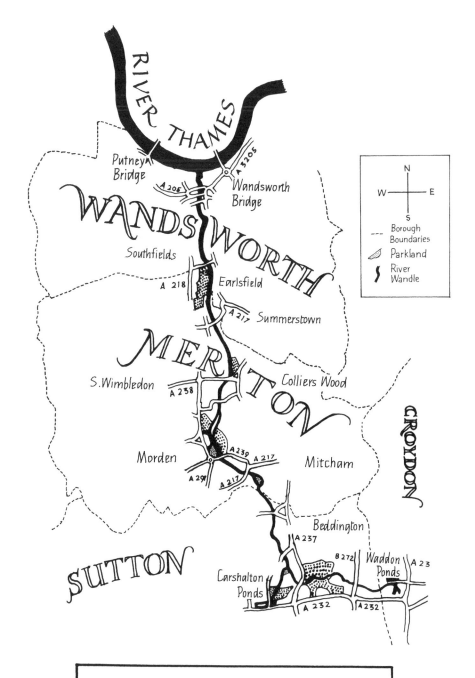

RIVER THAMES

Putney Bridge

A 205

Wandsworth Bridge

A 3205

WANDSWORTH

Southfields

A 218

Earlsfield

A 217 Summerstown

MERTON

S. Wimbledon

A 238

Colliers Wood

Morden

A 239 A 217

A 29

A 217

Mitcham

CROYDON

Beddington

A 237

B 272 Waddon Ponds A 23

SUTTON

Carshalton Ponds

A 232 A 232

N
W E
S

Borough Boundaries

Parkland

River Wandle

THE RIVER WANDLE

The Wandle Guide

by The Wandle Group

Edited by

Doug Cluett and John Phillips

sponsored by Thames Water

Sutton Leisure Services

First published 1997

by London Borough of Sutton Leisure Services

Central Library, St. Nicholas Way

Sutton, Surrey, SM1 1EA

© Text: London Borough of Sutton and the Wandle Group, 1997.

ISBN: 0 907335 33 0

Designed by Shirley Edwards.

Printed in Great Britain by Drogher Press, Christchurch, UK.

Contents

	Page
Foreword	4
Acknowledgements	5
List of Illustrations	6
Illustrations Acknowledgements	8
Introduction	9
The Wandle Trail	10
Croydon	11
Sutton	16
Merton	33
Wandsworth	44
The Geology of the River	53
Archaeology	55
Ecclesiastical establishments	57
Historic Houses	58
Industrial History	63
Natural History	68
Selective Bibliography	77

Foreword

We are delighted to support the publication of this excellent new guide to the River Wandle.

The health of the river is dependent on many factors but one of the most crucial is the quality of the water returned to it. Thames Water, as the largest water and sewerage company in the country, is well aware of its responsibilities to the environment and takes the issue of waste water quality very seriously.

Since privatisation, we have invested £500 million to improve the performance of our sewage treatment works and we will continue to invest well in the future to meet stringent standards for the clean water returned to rivers. In fact, overall river quality has improved by 35% since 1990.

We are proud of the contribution that we have made to the substantial and sustained improvements to the Wandle, and hope that our efforts will add to the enjoyment of the readers of this guide

John Sexton
Environment and Science Director
Thames Water Utilities

Acknowledgements

This book is a completely new revision of *The River Wandle: a Guide and Handbook*, edited by Royston Twilley and Professor Michael Wilks from material supplied by themselves and other members of The Wandle Group, and published in 1974.

The Wandle Group, formed one year before, in 1973, had been set up to co-ordinate the activities of organisations interested in the River Wandle from all points of view; and to facilitate liaison between them.

The 'Wandle Guide' as this publication was often called, was the first guide to the river for fifty years. The contributors to the first edition were: D.J.S. Cluett, J Jackson, the late Miss E.M. Jowett, A.R. Knight, K. Mercer, the late R.A. Michell, C.J. Monk, E.N. Montague, R.A. Shaw, W. Sibthorpe, P. Sowan, C.A. Toase, D. J. Turner, R.C. Twilley and Professor M.J. Wilks.

Of these, Doug Cluett, Eric Montague, Tony Shaw, Dennis Turner and Michael Wilks have worked on the present project, together with: Derek Bradford; Derek Coleman, Margaret Cunningham, Gwyneth Fookes, Mark Hodgins, Sally Peake, Colin Saunders, and Andrew Skelton.

Editorial help from Valary Murphy (Museum and Historic Houses Officer, Sutton Leisure Services) is acknowledged with thanks, as is the design by Shirley Edwards, who designed the original book.

Thames Water is to be thanked for its generous contribution towards the cost of publishing this Guide.

Doug Cluett (Chairman, Wandle Group)
John Phillips (Heritage Manager, Sutton Leisure Services)
Editors

List of Illustrations

		Page
1.	The boat-house in Wandle Park Croydon, around 1900.	14
2.	Waddon Ponds which formerly retained water for Waddon Mill.	15
3.	Beddington Mill.	17
4.	Mount Pleasant Cottages, Beddington c.1900.	18
5.	Sweeping duckweed from the cress beds at Guy Road, Beddington.	19
6.	Harvesting watercress at Guy Road, Beddington.	19
7.	The new wildlife pond to the east of Carew Manor, Beddington.	21
8.	Boating on the lake at Grange Park, Wallington, in 1956.	23
9.	Volunteers working on a Wandle clean-up day in 1987.	23
10.	The water-wheels of Ansell's snuff mills, Butterhill, Carshalton, c.1900.	28
11.	The iron bridge at Hackbridge.	30
12.	Pestles for grinding tobacco into snuff, at Lambert's Mill at Hackbridge, in the early 20th century.	32
13.	The upstream side of the mills above Goat Bridge.	33
14.	Skins hanging out to dry near Deed's leather mill, Mitcham.	34
15.	Deed's leather mill at Mitcham, c.1962.	34
16.	The Fishermen's Cottages, above Mitcham Bridge.	35
17.	Glover's snuff mill and Mitcham Bridge in the early 19th century.	36
18.	Ravensbury Mills in 1976.	37
19.	The snuff mills in Morden Hall Park.	39
20.	The Wandle from the Lydden Road Bridge, Earlsfield, c.1974.	44
21.	Engineering work at Penwith Road Bridge, Earlsfield in 1958.	45
22.	The Wandle at Strathville Road, Wandsworth, in 1958, when the river was at its worst.	46
23.	The Wandle from Buckhold Bridge, Wandsworth.	48

24. Cutting osiers (willows) at an unknown Wandleside
      location, c.1870-80.   50
25. The Wandle flowing into the Thames at Wandsworth.   52
26. The ponds at Carshalton in 1896.   59
27. The Culvers.   61
28. Merton Place, once the home of Lord Nelson.   62
29. The Pontifex Copper Mill, below Plough Lane Bridge,
      South Wimbledon, in the early 19th century.   64
30. The terminus of the Surrey Iron Railway at Wandsworth
      Basin in the early 19th century.   65
31. The wheel at Liberty's Mill, Merton, in 1976.   67
32 & 33.   Old and new riverbanks, from the footbridge at
      Richmond Green, Beddington.   69
34. Swans and cygnets at The Grove, Carshalton in 1954.   71
35. Volunteers working on a new wildlife pond on the site of
      the former Wandle Valley Hospital, 1986.   75
36. The Wandle at Spencer Road, Hackbridge.   76

Illustrations Acknowledgements

The majority of the illustrations in this book are reproduced from photographs in the collection of the London Borough of Sutton Heritage Service. We would like to thank the following people for permission to reproduce photographs:
22: N.C. Langridge; 27, 29: Frank Burgess; 24, 31, 36: J. Jackson.

Introduction

The river Wandle is a nine-mile-long tributary of the river Thames, which is fed by springs in the London Boroughs of Croydon and Sutton, which lie at the foot of the North Downs. It flows through the London Borough of Merton and meets the Thames at Wandsworth. It falls, on average, about fourteen feet per mile, being steepest in its upper reaches. This has always made the river useless for navigation, but very efficient for supplying water-power to mills. It supplied power not only for corn-milling, but also for making or working copper, iron, oil, leather, paper, snuff and gunpowder; and for printing textiles: and it was, therefore, important to London's economy. The river was once a famous trout stream, but has since suffered from industrial and other pollution. The river reached a low point in the 1950s. The turning point was probably the construction of a new sewage works at Beddington in the 1960s. Since then much hard work has been done to improve the quality of the river, and in recent years various improvements have been made at the Beddington works. Nowadays the river has two main sources: in Croydon (Waddon Ponds) and Carshalton (the Town Ponds). Although the underground water table is now much lower than in previous centuries, many higher springs, or bournes, still flow after long periods of heavy rainfall.

Before the late medieval period the river was called, among other variants of the name, the Ledeborne (recorded in 1230) and Lovebourn (1349) which are derived from the middle Saxon *Hlidaburne*, meaning either the loud (*hlyde*) or sloping (*hlid*) stream. Either reading may be appropriate to a river with the relatively sharp drop of about 4 metres (14ft) per mile over its total length. The present name appears to have been in use by the 16th century; Camden, the Elizabethan antiquarian, attempted to latinize it as 'Vandalis' in 1586. This does not justify the common assumption that 'Vandalis' was the original Roman name of the river and, whilst it has appeared on some maps, it is mostly poets who have made use of this variation.

THE WANDLE TRAIL

Since the first edition of the Wandle Guide was published, more and more people have been walking beside the river, and in 1988 this was formalised by the establishment of the Wandle Trail, a 12-mile route that follows the river as closely as possible. At the time of writing, about seventy-five percent of the riverside was accessible, with more due to come "on-line" in the near future. Much of it is already sign-posted.

The Wandle Group and its members, especially the Wandle Industrial Museum and the Ramblers' Association, have actively campaigned for the Trail to be set up and improved, with the eventual aim of receiving the "kitemark" of the London Walking Forum. With the co-operation of all four London Boroughs along the route (Croydon, Sutton, Merton and Wandsworth), the further improvements required to achieve this award are gradually being implemented.

Even now, the Wandle Trail is an important link in the extensive London Walking Network. At its northern end in Wandsworth, it will join the proposed Thames Path National Trail; at its southern end is the Vanguard Way which goes from Croydon to Seaford. Enterprising walkers can use these routes (and the Newhaven-Dieppe ferry) to walk from London to Paris!

The logical way to walk is with the flow of the river - from south to north - and our notes have been written in this direction. This has the added advantage of being downhill, though the incline is so gradual that those walking north to south will hardly notice it.

There are ample opportunities for refreshment and toilet stops all the way - these are detailed in italics in the route description.. A number of diversions and alternative routes are described in separate boxes. The route is well served by public transport: information on links to railway stations is provided within the route description, and buses cross the route at many points.

Public car parks are not very frequent, but they can be found in Central Croydon, at Beddington Park; Carshalton; Morden; Merton Abbey Mills, and Wandsworth. If you decide to park in the street, check any restrictions, and make sure that you are not blocking access to any-one's property or business.

Most of the Trail uses hard-surfaced paths or pavements suitable for wheelchairs and buggies. You can assume that the surface is suitable unless otherwise indicated in the route description. The following sections of the Trail may pose difficulty for the reasons shown:

> Beddington Park (mostly grass or mud; shallow steps on the footbridge across lake)
> The Watermeads (rough, narrow path. A hard-surface diversion is available)
> Ravensbury Park (muddy path)
> Morden Hall Park (footbridge with thirty steps over railway line)
> Wandle Meadow Nature Park (rough and muddy paths)
> Wandle Mouth (very narrow footbridge and barrier)

The start of the trail in the London Borough of Croydon

East Croydon station is served by bus or train from most parts of Central and South London. There are several multi-storey car parks in the town centre, and a very wide range of refreshment facilities.

The Trail starts at East Croydon station, where it joins the Vanguard Way leading to the Sussex coast. Outside the main entrance, turn right along George Street for 250 yards, then cross the dual carriageway and underpass at the traffic lights. Here, a little to your left along Park Lane, among the towering buildings of Croydon's modern business centre, you see the Fairfield Halls. An abrupt change of surroundings, with older and more human-sized buildings, heralds your continuation along George Street for 150 yards, passing Allders. *(Toilets in the Whitgift Centre through Allders' Mall.)*

At the next junction, you have the High Street to your left and the pedestrianised North End to your right. Here, you are at the heart of the ancient town of Croydon, with the Hospital of the Holy Trinity, one of the town's oldest buildings, on your right. Sometimes known as the Whitgift Hospital, these alms-houses were established by Archbishop Whitgift in 1596 and survive as an oasis of calm in a bustling community.

West Croydon railway and bus stations are 600 yards north of this point, (to the right). From the railway station, turn left and walk ahead along the pedestrianised North End. From the bus station, turn left to the junction with North End, then left again.

The land now starts to drop away into the Wandle valley. Carry straight on down the steep but short Crown Hill. At its foot, go a little to the left and walk along the narrow, cobbled Bell Hill - it is all that remains of a clutch of similar streets that once characterised this area. At the end is Surrey Street, which from Mondays to Saturdays hosts a bustling market. Note the old shops whose upper storeys extend out over the pavement; they were once part of a much longer terrace called The Shambles.

At the end of Bell Hill, turn right, then immediately left, into Church Street, which curves gracefully round to the right. The buildings are mostly quite old, but have been spoiled by modern shop fascias. In 150 yards, by the Gun Tavern *(toilets in the In-Shops shopping arcade)*, turn left along Old Palace Road, named after Croydon Palace, much of which remains and forms part of the Old Palace School.

The Palace formerly belonged to the Archbishops of Canterbury, who owned the manor of Croydon by 871. In the Middle Ages the Palace was of considerable importance, as it provided a house close to London, and was used as the administrative headquarters of the Archbishops' estates in Surrey, Middlesex and Hertfordshire. The palace fell from favour in the 18th century, apparently due to its unhealthy situation amid watercourses which were, no doubt, heavily polluted with sewage from the town. The buildings were used as a printing and bleaching works. In 1887 it was bought and turned into a school. The most important part of the building is the Great Hall, which dates from the 15th century. There is also a 15th century guard room and a Tudor long gallery and domestic chapel.

Turn right into Church Road. (Before you turn note the long, three-storey building on the left hand side a little further along Old Palace Road. This was formerly the original warehouse of the Pickfords removals company.) You now enter one of Croydon's conservation areas. In a few yards, by some telephone kiosks, turn left, off Church Road, along a passage which leads through the churchyard of Croydon Parish Church. On your right, as you enter the passage, is a row of flint-walled, timber-framed buildings known as The Gothic Villas, which stand on part of the site of the palace stables.

In front of the main entrance of the church, you can choose between a subway and a pedestrian crossing to take you under or across Old Town. On the far side, keep ahead along St. John's Road for a short distance to a five-ways junction, where you turn right along Sylverdale Road, a cul-de-sac. At its end, go left through a short, narrow passage, then right, along Ridge's Yard to Waddon New Road.

Cross the road then turn right for fifty yards to a footbridge over the railway (with steps) which takes you into Wandle Park, the first of two parks bearing this name along the Trail.

(If the Croydon Tramlink scheme comes into being, the footbridge will be moved to a point opposite Ridge's Yard. The steps can be avoided by turning left along Waddon New Road to the traffic lights, then sharp right along Waddon Road and over the railway to rejoin the route at Vicarage Road.) Inside the park, turn left and follow the railway line (passing toilets).

Just beyond the footbridge, you can see the point where the Wandle once flowed under the railway line (it is now in a culvert). At the beginning of this century there was a lake in this park which was used for boating. It was filled in in 1964 and the river from here to Waddon Ponds is now culverted.

Cross the steeply-ramped footbridge (which is due to be replaced by a Tramlink stop) into Vicarage Road, and go along it to Waddon Road. Turn right for 300 yards to the traffic lights, and cross Purley Way, keeping ahead along Mill Lane for 200 yards to Waddon Ponds. (1 mile)

1. The boat-house in Wandle Park Croydon, around 1900. This lake was created as an amenity in the park, and was filled in during the 1960s, after it had been dry for some time.

Although the river now normally first flows in the open at this point, higher sources such as the Merstham and Caterham bournes can be seen flowing after prolonged periods of heavy rain. When these bournes flow, they join near Purley Railway Station, and pass underground along the line of the Brighton Road into central Croydon and down to Wandle Park.

There were once two ponds here, the existing one to the south of the road, and another to the north, which was filled-in when the river upstream was culverted in 1964. However, the delightful small park that surrounds the remaining pond retains the plural name *(toilets on left hand side)*. The park was once part of the grounds of Waddon Court, a house that stood at the south end of the ponds. Waddon Mill stood where the river flowed out of the northern pond, turning its wheel as it went. It was probably an ancient mill site. In 1792 it was rebuilt as a flour mill to the designs of the great 18th century engineer John Smeaton, who is best known for the construction of the third Eddystone Light House. In the 19th century the mill was rebuilt as a large brick factory which had its own siding running north to the Croydon-Wimbledon railway.

2.   Waddon Ponds which formerly retained water for Waddon Mill.

__Link route from Waddon railway station, 400 yards from Waddon Ponds.__ Buses from Croydon, Sutton, Carshalton and Morden also stop nearby. The nearest public car parks to Waddon Ponds are in Central Croydon. From Waddon station (refreshments: The Waddon pub), turn right to the main road, Purley Way (the busy junction nearby is known locally as Five Ways), then right again for 75 yards to cross Purley Way at the pedestrian lights just past the junctions with Croydon Road, Waddon Court Road and Waddon Park Avenue. Go down Waddon Court Road for 50 yards, then turn left into the park, which is also called Waddon Ponds. Turn right by the pond to emerge into Mill Lane, where you turn left. The two tall brick chimneys ahead surmount the Ikea store, and were formerly part of a power station. If the park is closed, instead of going ahead along Waddon Court Road, turn left along Court Drive, then right along The Ridgeway, at the end of which is a public footpath leading ahead to Mill Lane.

The river goes under Mill Lane and flows under the commercial estate built over the north pond. The Wandle Trail continues from the end of Mill Lane via the right-hand footpath. One hundred and fifty yards along the path, the river emerges on your right, and at this point you leave Croydon and enter the London Borough of Sutton. The boundary also separated Croydon and Beddington Parishes and was known as the Mere Bank, a Saxon name meaning boundary bank.

London Borough of Sutton

Shortly after the bank, the path joins the end of Aldwick Road, where a number of Late Bronze Age and Iron Age finds have been made. Continue for a further 150 yards along the path, then cross the footbridge over the river and immediately turn left to follow the north bank along Richmond Green - there were watercress beds here until the 1930s. In 200 yards, where the road swings right, keep ahead along a riverside footpath (to left of house number 13). At this point, the river divides into two channels - the left-hand one was the millstream and it passes under the former Beddington Mill. This was probably on the site of a medieval mill, and, in the early 17th century, it was used for grinding corn. By 1805 a Mr Williamson was using it to grind tobacco into snuff. He was followed by the Lambert family, who made snuff on the site until they moved to Hackbridge in the second half of the 1870s. The mill subsequently reverted to corn grinding. The existing brick mill was built in the 1890s for J. and T.H. Wallis, who ran a bakery as well as a flour mill. The adjacent mill house to the south of it is much older.

On reaching Wandle Road, turn left, then very soon turn right (opposite the miller's house with red descriptive plaque) along Bridges Lane, passing the Mount Pleasant Cottages on the opposite bank, which were built in 1884 to house mill workers.

Go along the riverside footpath to the very busy main road (Beddington Lane / Hilliers Lane) - cross with extreme caution. This section of river was once a ford, and carts also went along the river bed to the mill.

The two channels unite in a small open space on the far side of the main road. Continue along the river for a short distance and then cross the footbridge to the north bank and continue downstream. The grassed area was once watercress beds. Follow the river as it swings

3. Beddington Mill. The tall brick building dates from the 1890s and replaced an earlier wooden structure. The mill house to the right of it probably dates from the 17th or 18th century.

4. Mount Pleasant Cottages, Beddington c. 1900. These were built for mill workers in the 1870s. The house on the left is Wandle Court, which was demolished c. 1930.

right. The pond on the other side of the river was constructed by the National Rivers Authority in 1992, for flood relief and wildlife amenity purposes.

Here you have a view of Carew Manor behind the pond. The exterior of this building mostly dates from the 1860s when it was turned from a country house to an orphanage. Before that it was for five centuries the home of the Carews of Beddington, and their heirs, and the house still contains a Great Hall with an impressive timber arch-braced hammer-beam roof which dates from around 1500. In the Elizabethan period, Sir Francis Carew constructed a magnificent garden to the east of the house. The river flowed through it in a series of channels which were decorated with fountains, grottoes, a mount or artificial rock, and several toy ships and mills. This garden was remodelled at the beginning of the 18th century, when two lakes were laid out, one on the site of the large willows to the east of the house, and one along the tree-lined avenue to the west. Parts of the 18th century brick garden walls can still be seen, together with the ornamental 'Orangery Wall' which formed the north side of the reconstructed orange-house, a predecessor

5. Sweeping duckweed from the cress beds at Guy Road, Beddington.

6. Harvesting watercress at Guy Road, Beddington.

of the modern greenhouse. The brick structure replaced a wooden orange-house which had been built by Francis Carew in the second half of the 16th century.

The river now turns left and the Trail crosses a grassy field (muddy in places), then, after crossing the river on a short, hard-surfaced bridge, it crosses a second grassy/muddy playing field towards a group of red brick cottages. You now enter Beddington Park.

Wheelchairs and buggies can easily avoid the muddy section beyond the flood relief pond by continuing along the hard-surfaced path away from the river to Mallinson Road, where you turn left, then immediately right, into Crispin Crescent. In 50 yards, turn left along a footpath between the houses - this soon leads to the north bank of the river, and on to rejoin the Wandle Trail route opposite the group of red-brick cottages.

Passing round the north side of the cottages, you come to a bridge over the Wandle, which you cross, then turn left along a park road. Carew Manor, its Dovecote, East Lodge, and Beddington Church, dominate the scene to your left. *(Refreshments in the church on summer Sundays).*

The dovecote dates from the early 18th century, and has nesting boxes for 1360 pigeons, which were reared for food. East Lodge was built in 1877 for Canon Bridges, the wealthy rector of Beddington, who acquired the park after the last of the Hallowell-Carews had been forced, in 1859, to sell the estate to pay gambling debts. The lodge stood at the then entrance to the park and presumably housed a keeper.

After a short distance, you come to an ornamental terracotta bridge, which was made for Canon Bridges by the Watcombe Pottery, Torquay. The bridge was badly damaged when a tree fell on it in the gale of 1987, and has been considerably restored.

(Toilets including disabled: turn right to follow the park road northwards for 200 yards to the sports pavilion.) Continue through the park beside the north bank of the river, now on grass, with a section through

7.   The new wildlife pond to the east of Carew Manor, Beddington.

a copse that can be muddy. The river bends a couple of times, then, after 500 yards, you reach a flint bridge, with The Grange, a 'Henry's Table' pub/restaurant away to your right. The latter stands on the site of a house called The Grange, which was built around 1880 for Alfred Hutchison Smee, whose father, Alfred, had constructed a magnificent garden on the site. Parts of the Victorian rockery survive by the lake, and there are some other garden remnants, but the house was burnt down in January 1960.

The lake originally served as the pond for Wallington Mill, which is first recorded in the 18th century, when it was used for paper making. In the early 19th century it was being used for calico bleaching and printing. Later it was a flour mill, then a paper mill again, and it ended its life as part of a chocolate factory.

Continue until you reach London Road *(buses to Carshalton and Wallington; there is a small car park here).*

On either side of the river at this point are two interesting old buildings: on the east bank is Bridge House (c. 1770) which was attached to Wallington Mill, whilst an early 18th century house called Wandle

Bank lies on the west side. The latter was the home of the artist Arthur Hughes from 1876 to 1891. He was associated with the Pre-Raphaelite group of painters; and the room with the large windows at the river end of the house was added as his studio.

There is a spring-fed pool, on the east side of London Road, which is maintained as a small park and can be visited by a short detour.

Beyond London Road, the Wandle flows between private properties, with no public access for the last 600 yards of its journey to the confluence of the Waddon and Carshalton branches. This enforced diversion provides the Wandle Trail walker with an opportunity to visit Carshalton - one not to be missed as there is much of interest - and to pick up the other main branch of the river at Carshalton Ponds.

Turn left and go uphill along London Road to the Rose and Crown public house. At this point, those not wishing to visit Carshalton can take a short cut (saving nearly three quarters of a mile) by turning right in front of the pub, and going down Butter Hill. The route to Carshalton is along Westcroft Road, a side turning which is more or less straight ahead.

(2 miles)

Continue ahead along Westcroft Road. After 250 yards, turn right towards the Westcroft Sports and Leisure Centre, and then turn left into the park over a wooden bridge which crosses the Westcroft Canal. This is normally dry, but in the past it brought water from Carshalton Park to The Grove Mill, which stood near the Wandle above Butter Hill bridge. In the late 18th and early 19th centuries the mill ground tobacco into snuff. It was later used as an iron-works, but it was burnt down in the early 1950s; and the site is now given over to housing.

Keep ahead on the hard-surfaced path to a junction beside a crazy-golf course. The Trail goes right here, but you can turn left for the facilities in Carshalton High Street *(refreshments: several pubs, cafes etc.; automatic toilet).*

A Diversion to Carshalton Park, Honeywood, Margaret's Pool, and Carshalton House.

11.   Boating on the lake at Grange Park, Wallington, in 1956. The building in the background is The Grange, which was burnt down in 1960.

This pleasant and interesting diversion can be made from Carshalton High Street. Cross at the lights beside the Fox and Hounds pub, then turn right, walk along the High Street for 75 yards, and then turn left into Carshalton Place. The channel on the left (normally dry) is an upstream section of the Westcroft Canal which you can follow all the way into Carshalton Park, crossing Talbot Road, then Ruskin Road, and eventually reaching The Grotto, from which issues (after periods of prolonged rainfall) the Grotto Canal, which becomes the Westcroft Canal, and is at such times another source of the Wandle. The route beside the canal within the park is on grass, so wheelchairs and buggies may have to divert to use the path to the right.

The grotto probably dates from 1725, and was built as part of the gardens around the now demolished Carshalton Park House. It stands over springs which flowed out of the three small culverts which can be seen at water level. The large opening above the culverts leads to the main grotto chamber, which probably contained a fountain. The structure was originally covered with flint, glass waste, and imitation coral. The latter was cast in lead, and painted red, so that it would have looked very gaudy.

Climb the steps to the right of the Grotto, then turn right on a hard-surfaced path diagonally across the park. You pass to your left the extraordinary, deep and reservoir-like Hogpit Pond, another Wandle source when the water-table is unusually high. *(Toilets on right by tennis courts - may be closed.)* The name Hog Pit can be traced back to the mid-15th century. It may originally have been a quarry, and was probably given its current form in the 18th century, when it was altered to form a reservoir to supply a mill by the Coach and Horses at Carshalton Ponds, and to feed some extra water into the Westcroft Canal for The Grove Mill. Continue to the park's main entrance on Ruskin Road, which you cross, then keep ahead along a pink, paved path which leads down to a road called The Square. Continue ahead, passing what is believed to be the Orangery of the former Carshalton Park House, on your right) to rejoin the High Street. Carshalton Ponds are to your left, but crossing the very busy road at this point can be difficult and dangerous, so if you wish to rejoin the main Wandle Trail you should go a little to your right to cross at the lights.

Otherwise, turn left to pass the Coach and Horses public house, through whose cellars flows the stream feeding the Wandle from the Hogpit Pond. Next door is the Woodman wine bar, partly 15th century, once a butcher's shop; and one of Carshalton's oldest and most picturesque buildings. Behind it in the churchyard is a timber-framed cottage. The church itself is partly 12th century, and on its west side in Church Hill lies 'Anne Boleyn's Well' the name of which may derive from a medieval dedication to 'Our Lady of Boulogne' - a cult of the Virgin Mary which may have been promoted locally when Faramus, Count of Boulogne, was Lord of the Manor of Carshalton, in the 12th century.

Continue past the Greyhound Hotel, and keep ahead into Pound Street. Cross the road beyond the Greyhound and notice Margaret's Pool (normally dry) at the corner of Pound Street and West Street. In the 19th century the pool came to the attention of John Ruskin, who complained, in the introduction to his book *A Crown of Wild Olive*, published in 1872, that the inhabitants of Carshalton defiled the Wandle springs by casting "their street and house foulness, heaps of dust and slime, and broken shreds of old metal, and rags of putrid cloths..." into them. Ruskin had the pool cleaned, and had seven tons of stone

9.   Volunteers working on a Wandle clean-up day in 1987. An activity which would have won the approval of John Ruskin (see page 24)

brought from Coniston, in the Lake District, to decorate the edges. The pool passed into the hands of Carshalton Urban District Council, who extended it southwards towards Pound Street, around 1920, when the old Police Station there was demolished.

Return down the north side of Pound Street, to the Ponds. On the corner is Honeywood, which houses the London Borough of Sutton's Heritage Centre. Honeywood's exhibitions include a permanent one on the Wandle, and it has good tea-rooms. Water sometimes flows in the culvert under the house from springs in Margaret's Pool and the channel leading from it. When the springs in the ponds are not flowing, water is pumped back from the Wandle below Goat Bridge, and flows into the ponds in front of the house. The installation of this system was a planning requirement when new Wandle-water-robbing wells were sunk in the 1960s by Sutton District Water Company.

Go down the north side of the pond (Honeywood Walk) past the war memorial. Cross North Street and go through a pedestrian gate in the brick wall of The Grove park. Go ahead under the low branch of the splendid cedar tree to rejoin the main route of the Wandle Trail at the white stone 'Leoni Bridge'.

After turning right beside the crazy-golf course, continue through The Grove passing to your right The Grove house. *(Toilets on left.)* This was built in the mid-19th century and was considerably enlarged around the turn of the century.

You now reach Carshalton Ponds. There are, in fact, two ponds separated by the North Street causeway and bridge. In the 17th century there was a line of springs along the south side of the Lower Pond, next to the churchyard, and the water from these flowed across a piece of boggy ground to a small pond. The two existing ponds were probably created at some point in the early 18th century by raising the dam of Upper Mill so that the water was penned back and flooded the area. At the beginning of the 19th century the causeway across the ponds was pedestrian only, and vehicles had to ford through the water. The same applied to the road along the south side of the pond by the churchyard, until the existing brick-sided causeways were built in the 1820s. The white stone bridge where the river leaves the ponds dates from the 18th century, and is often attributed to the Italian architect Giacomo Leoni, although there is no firm evidence for this. It bears the griffin from the arms of the Scawen family, who lived in Stone Court, a large house which stood on the west side of the river, 100 yards downstream.

A short diversion for tea
At this point you can make a short diversion to Honeywood, the Heritage Centre which stands opposite the Greyhound at the western end of Upper Pond. This contains displays on the Wandle and other aspects of local history, and also has tea rooms.

Go to the white, stone, 'Leoni Bridge' where the Wandle flows out of the Ponds. **The diversion to Carshalton Park rejoins at this point.** The Trail now continues along the right-hand side of the river as you look downstream.

Before you turn, you can hardly miss seeing, on the path ahead, the limb of an ancient cedar tree spreading at head height across the path and over the pond.

For Carshalton railway station, go under this tree, through a doorway in the brick wall into North Street, then turn right for 300 yards. Buses to Croydon, Sutton, Morden, Mitcham.

Go downstream for about 100 yards. The buildings on the opposite side of the river now comprise Stone Court. This was an ancient sub-manor of Carshalton. There was a substantial house on the site in the late Middle Ages. The house was rebuilt around 1710 and was quite a grand mansion. It was acquired by the Scawen family, who were one of the major Carshalton land owners for much of the 18th century. The house was demolished in the early 19th century, and the outbuildings were converted into a smaller residence which, with later modifications, survives as offices. In the 19th century The Grove became the main house on the estate.

Continue until you reach a cascade, and then cross the footbridge to Upper Mill. This is an ancient mill site which can be traced back to the Middle Ages. In 1782 it was rebuilt as a flour mill to the designs of John Smeaton. The existing stone wheel-pits date from this time. The flour mill was demolished in 1887 and the alpine-style wooden building erected to house the generator for an early private electricity supply for The Grove and Stone Court. It was initially powered by a water-wheel, but this was superseded by a turbine around 1900. The site is currently being restored.

Go back over the bridge and continue beside the river, then bear left and cross the river over a brick bridge. Follow the path downstream between the houses and the river. Cross Paper Mill Close, once the site of a paper mill and latterly a chemical works, then continue along the river bank until the path turns to the left and enters Mill Lane. Turn right, and after a short distance you will come to Butter Hill Bridge, which dates from 1787 but has been heavily rebuilt. The row of buildings along the west side of the river, above the bridge, can be traced back to at least the early 19th century, and once housed Ansell's snuff mill. There was another small mill on the east bank of the river, which

10.   The water-wheels of Ansell's snuff mills, Butterhill, Carshalton, around 1900.
Part of the buildings of Denyer's flour mill can be seen top left.

was also used by Ansell. If you look upstream from the bridge you can see the site of the two water-wheel pits which once stood in the channel. A third mill, which was latterly used for corn-grinding, stood just east of the river.

Return to Mill Lane and continue along it, passing under the railway bridge, which dates from 1868. At the corner of Strawberry Lane is Strawberry Lodge, which was built in the late 17th century for the gunpowder maker Josias (or Josiah) Dewye, who operated the mills a short distance downstream . The Baptist Church, to which it belongs, has now converted it into a community centre, following a recent restoration.

Continue to follow the Wandle and go along River Gardens. A footbridge over the river leads on to Wilderness Island, which used to be a rubbish dump, but is now a nature reserve to which the public are admitted.

(3 miles)

In 150 yards, shortly after River Gardens swings left, turn right, along the riverside footpath. It shortly reaches the confluence of the Carshalton and Croydon branches of the Wandle, which unite as they plunge over a weir beneath your feet. This was a major mill site. In the late-17th century, Josias Dewye made gunpowder here. It was subsequently a copper mill. By the late 18th century George Shepley was operating oil and leather mills on the site. He was the principal promoter of the Surrey Iron Railway, the first public railway in the world; which ran from Wandsworth to Croydon, and was opened in 1803. (This was for freight not passengers.) It had horse-drawn wagons which were held on the track by flanged rails with an L shaped cross section. A branch ran to this mill from the main line at Beddington Corner.

The path continues to the left, with the river in culvert below. It reappears after a short distance. Continue beside it for 250 yards to the Hackbridge, linking Nightingale Road and Hackbridge Road. There was a bridge near this site in the Middle Ages which, around 1800, was replaced by an early example of an iron bridge. This was in turn replaced in 1912, and has subsequently been replaced again.

11. The iron bridge at Hackbridge. This was erected in the early 19th century, and survived until 1912.

(Refreshments: Old Red Lion pub - 100 yards east along Hackbridge Road). For Hackbridge railway station turn right, along Hackbridge Road, for 400 yards, then right again, along London Road for 200 yards. Buses to Mitcham, Wallington, Sutton, Carshalton.

Cross the bridge and turn immediately left along the riverside path on the east bank (keep to the left-hand track immediately next to the river; the right-hand one is for cyclists). Cross the white concrete footbridge, which leads to Culvers Island, formed by the river's division into two channels, with the eastern one now taking the main flow. In the late-18th and early-19th centuries, Culvers Island was used as a calico-bleaching ground. The industry went into decline after the invention of modern chemical bleaches, and the site was bought by the Quaker banker, Samuel Gurney, who built a house on the site, which has now been demolished.

When a planned footbridge is constructed, at the northern tip of the island, you will be able to continue from the concrete footbridge along the island side of the eastern channel. For the time being, though, you have to cross the island by continuing ahead from the footbridge, using the right-hand track of a joint foot/cycle-path which leads shortly to Culvers Retreat (a road). Turn right and go along the Retreat for 100 yards, to Culvers Avenue. Turn left, and after a few yards you can look over a low brick wall into the pit which once housed the water wheel for Culvers Mill. This was used for making flour, and two of the mill stones can be seen, set into the grass, at the junction with a road called Millside, just uphill on the left. *(Buses to Morden.)*

The river re-emerges on the north side of Culvers Avenue, opposite the wheel-pit, and the path continues along the west side, with a cycle track next to it. On the opposite bank is the site of the Mullards electronics factory, which has now been demolished, and its site used for a housing estate. Seven hundred yards after Culvers Avenue, you reach the head of another large island. The main, eastern, channel veers off to the right and you follow the western channel which is now normally dry. The land to your left was formerly occupied by the Wandle Valley Isolation Hospital and Mitcham Rugby Football Club.

(4 miles)

The yellow-brick house on the right, as you are approaching Middleton Road, formerly belonged to the owner of a large skinning mill, which stood behind it on the island. The mill is first recorded in the mid-18th century when it was operated by the Savignacs, who may have been of French origin. It was later operated by William McRae, and then his sons, who worked on the site until the 1880s. When you reach the road, walk on to Goat Bridge and look back up the main channel of the Wandle, which now flows down the east side of the island. In the 19th and early-20th centuries there were three mills on this channel. The skinning mill on the island, to the right, and a corn mill and a drug grinding mill on the east bank to the left. In the winter, when there are no leaves on the trees, you can look back upstream from the bridge and see the water flowing over the weir on the site of the mill wheels.

To your right, along Goat Road, lies Mill Green. There are three pubs around this, two of which, The Goat and the Skinners' Arms (recently renamed Hungry Horse), drew their names from the leather industry, which was formerly important in the area. *For Mitcham Junction Railway Station continue along the road to the Goat pub, then turn left and walk along Carshalton Road for 400 yards.*

12.   Pestles for grinding tobacco into snuff, at Lambert's Mill at Hackbridge, in the early 20th century.

Go back across the bridge to the west side of the river and continue along Watermead Lane. This contains a terrace of late-19th century cottages, which probably originally housed workers employed at an adjacent tannery. This was demolished many years ago, and the site is now covered with houses. After 150 yards, at the end of the lane, you continue along the riverside footpath; soon passing, on the opposite bank, machinery which, at times of low flow, pumps water back to Carshalton Ponds through a pipeline laid along the river bed. Immediately downstream, the outfall from the sewage treatment works in Beddington Lane discharges into the river.

The land on the opposite bank is the Willow Lane Industrial Estate in the borough of Merton. The land to your left is Poulter Park, with, at its far end, the house called Bishopsford, which was probably built in the 1860s for Alfred Attwood, who was a wholesale druggist and associate of George Meggeson, manufacturer of cough lozenges and

13.   The upstream side of the mills above Goat Bridge. The building on the left was
a leather mill; the large weather-boarded structure, a flour mill; while the wheel on
the far right powered a drug and dye mill.

'jujubes'. The river now bends sharply right and you leave the London
Borough of Sutton.

London Borough of Merton

The river bends at what, since medieval times, has been known as
Bennett's Hole or Hollow. The land on the opposite bank is now a
local nature reserve. A footbridge is planned to link with this, as well

14.   Skins hanging out to dry near Deed's leather mill, Mitcham.

15.   Deed's leather mill at Mitcham, c. 1962. This stood between Goat Bridge and
Mitcham Bridge.

16.   The Fishermen's Cottages, above Mitcham Bridge. Despite their name these were originally built for mill workers.

as with a new section of the Wandle Trail which will continue along the east bank northwards to London Road. For the present, though, the river turns to the right and the path leaves it. After a short distance you come to a metal fence which runs alongside The Watermeads, a National Trust nature reserve. (You can obtain access to this by contacting the National Trust warden's office at Morden Hall Park 0181-648 1845.) Continue beside the fence for 400 yards to Bishopsford Road. *Wheelchairs and buggies cannot use this path, but can continue along the hard-surfaced path which leads shortly to a park track and then on to Bishopsford Road. At the road turn right to rejoin the Trail by The Watermeads).* Just before Bishopsford Road you see on your right three white, weatherboarded mill cottages (in more recent times dubbed the Fishermen's or Fisheries Cottages) - the two oldest of which date from the 1700s.

(5 miles)

Turn right at Bishopsford Road, which becomes London Road at Mitcham Bridge. *For Mitcham Railway Station (which may become a stop on the Croydon Tramlink system), keep ahead for 300 yards. Refreshments: several pubs and cafes in Mitcham.*

After crossing Mitcham Bridge, remain on the right-hand pavement for

25.   Glover's snuff mill and Mitcham Bridge in the early 19th century.

50 yards to the corner of Riverside Drive, then cross London Road. (Wandle Grove, a fine late-18th century house, survives in Riverside Drive.) Go left through the gap at the end of the red brick wall and continue along the footpath which skirts The Watermeads housing estate on the site of a house called Mitcham Grove. Note the iron parish-boundary marker, dated 1882, fixed to the centre of the downstream side of the bridge.

Mitcham Grove appears to have been another 18th century house built on the site of a medieval one. In the 16th century the house on the site was the residence of Thomas Smythe, a court official to Elizabeth I. The house remained with his descendants until the mid-18th century. Lord Clive of India owned Mitcham Grove briefly before 1773, when he presented it to Sir Alexander Wedderburn, K.C., later Lord Loughborough, in recognition of Wedderburn's defence of him during House of Commons impeachment proceedings. It was purchased in 1786 by Henry Hoare, senior partner in Hoare's Bank. He was a relative of another Henry Hoare, also involved in the family bank, who built Stourhead in Wiltshire. After Hoare died, in 1828, the house was purchased by Sir John Lubbock; but, coming on the market again later,

18. Ravensbury Mills in 1976. These were once used for grinding tobacco into snuff. Part of the building will soon house the Wandle Industrial Museum.

Mitcham Grove failed to find a purchaser, and was, sadly, demolished by 1846. Known locally for many years as the Hovis sports ground, the land of Mitcham Grove was developed for housing by the London Borough of Merton in the mid-1970s.

The trail now goes across a metal footbridge over a branch of the river and continues along a small island with a pond on the right, a flood control feature which is in effect a small nature reserve. The cedar has survived from the grounds of Mitcham Grove. You next come to a second metal bridge and enter Ravensbury Park *(seasonal cafe; toilets including disabled)*. Turn left at the end of the bridge and continue along the side of the main river, which widens to make a pond for Ravensbury Mill. After a while you come to a footbridge over the river. Continue on the same bank to a metal bridge over an incoming side stream. Just before you cross the bridge you can see the yellow brick building of Ravensbury Mill, part of which is to become the Wandle Industrial Museum.

The path bears right, over the metal bridge, leaves the park, and joins the very busy Morden Road. Turn right to cross at a traffic island. *(Refreshments: Surrey Arms and Ravensbury Tavern pubs).*

The Trail continues through a gate, almost hidden, in the wooden fence just before the Surrey Arms. White Cottage, the weatherboarded house on the far side of the pub, is of 18th century date, and belongs to the National Trust (although not open to visitors). The wooden gate leads into Morden Hall Park (also National Trust). Inside, bear left immediately off the main avenue on a rough, sometimes muddy, footpath which leads back to the riverside (an alternative route follows the avenue of limes and chestnuts which eventually bears left to Morden Hall). On the opposite (western) bank of the river are the grounds of Morden Lodge, built around 1828 on the site of the earlier 'Regency' villa of Abraham Goldsmidt, a city financier. In 1810 he committed suicide on the wooded Wilderness Island which forms the far bank of the river.

Follow the river until a high red-brick wall is visible on the opposite bank. This once enclosed the kitchen garden of Morden Hall (which is now a garden centre). The path turns away from the river at this point, but you can do a short diversion downstream to view the back

19.   The snuff mills in Morden Hall Park.

of Morden Hall snuff mills, and a neat brick arch in the wall which allows a branch of the river to flow into the former kitchen garden.

Return to the main path, and continue along it until it meets a larger path in an avenue of lime trees. Go left here, over a small bridge, and walk towards Morden Hall, the large white building ahead.
(6 miles)

Cross the wooden footbridge, with decorative iron railings, over the main river channel. You can now turn left if you wish to see the snuff mills, or visit the National Trust's visitor centre, shop, and cafeteria (toilets available).

Morden Hall, an 18th century mansion built by Richard Garth, was bequeathed to the National Trust in 1941 under the will of Gilliat Edward Hatfeild, the last Lord of the Manor of Morden. The snuff mills, closed in 1922, date from the mid-18th century, and were in the hands of the Hatfeild family from 1854. The mansion, having been used for some years as offices by the London Borough of Merton, is now a 'Beefeater' restaurant and pub. It has little of its original interior remaining.

The Trail continues to the right, crossing two more footbridges - note the moat and remains of decorative brick bridges to your left. After the second bridge, fork right and cross a third bridge to rejoin the main river channel. Follow the made-up path and the signs to Deen City Farm, recently re-established here from a former site in Church Road, Mitcham. (The name derives from farm's original presence in Aber<u>deen</u> Road, Thornton Heath, Croydon.) When you come to the railway line, turn right and go over the footbridge. *(For Morden Station on the Northern Line, and buses in all directions, go left here to leave the park, and cross Morden Road, keeping ahead along London Road for 300 yards. To reach Morden Road Railway Station (due to become a stop on the Croydon Tramlink network), turn right outside the park gate, and proceed northwards along Morden Road for 300 yards.*

Having crossed the railway line, follow the path and then turn right, over a little bridge crossing a ditch, into Bunce's Meadow, which also belongs to the National Trust. Here the path meets the main channel of the Wandle. Follow the river downstream to the end of Bunce's Meadow, where Deen City Farm is now located. Here the river is joined by a parallel channel known as Rucker's Cut, after a calico printer who had it dug in 1769. Cross Phipps Bridge and turn right to make a short detour to see Wandle Villa (c.1788), and its Gothic lodge. Everett's Place (a row of old cottages dated 1824) is buttressed by a folly of about 1870. All these properties are owned by the National Trust, but are privately occupied and not open to the public.

With an overhead power line for company, the Wandle Trail continues alongside the west bank of the river, following a wide, hard-surfaced roadway for 200 yards to Windsor Avenue. There is also a narrow grassy path along the east bank - it crosses a small sluice marking the start of the Pickle Ditch - which follows the former line of the river round the east side of Merton Priory. After Windsor Avenue, keep ahead on the path, passing on the opposite bank a second, larger sluice leading to Bennett's Ditch. The origin of this watercourse is unknown, but it was already in existence in the 1740s. Its present name perpetuates the memory of Thomas Bennett, who had a calico-printing works here early in the 19th century. In 300 yards you reach the entrance to Merton Abbey Mills *(pub, cafes, toilets),* behind which the remains of the Chapter House of Merton Priory can be viewed through glass panels beneath Merantun Way, and are sometimes accessible by arrangement on weekend guided visits.

The great Augustinian priory of Merton, dedicated in 1117, received its charter in 1121. It continued to enjoy royal patronage throughout the Middle Ages, but was dissolved by Henry VIII in 1538. Much of the masonry from the church was used in the building of Nonsuch Palace, but parts of various buildings survived on the site until early in the 20th century. Little now remains to be seen above ground, but extensive evidence was exposed during archaeological excavations in the 1970s and 1980s.

In 1724, a calico printing works was established within the priory precinct wall, and the site remained occupied by textile-printing firms until the early 1980s. Liberty and Co. of Regent Street took over the site in the 19th century, and continued into the 20th century.

Cross Merantun Way at the pedestrian lights, go through a new brick arch (erected between sections of the ancient boundary wall of Merton Priory), then bear half right across the old road to join a riverside path, opened in 1991. Note the stone-block wall, which may be medieval, along the opposite side of the river channel. Previously, this section of the Wandle had been enclosed within an industrial site, and the path was included in the development of the Savacentre superstore *(cafe, toilets)* which dominates the opposite (east) bank. A short distance along the west bank, just before the Savacentre footbridge, there are some new flats which occupy the site of William Morris's 'Merton Abbey Print Works'.

(7 miles)

On reaching the main entrance to the Savacentre, at the time of writing, you must cross Merton High Street *(pubs, several cafes)* then turn right along it for 100 yards to Merton Bridge. The Savacentre occupies the site of the priory's 'Amery Mills'. A copper mill was working here throughout the 18th and for much of the 19th century. It was followed by Merton Board Mills, demolished in 1985 after a fire.

The Pickle Ditch rejoins the main river at the far end of the Savacentre, next to a further length of the priory wall, owned by the National Trust. It is hoped that it will eventually be possible to walk along a footpath on the south bank outside the Savacentre, then cross on a planned footbridge by the confluence with the Pickle Ditch.

Continue downstream along Wandle Bank (a road alongside the river), noting the early 19th century cottages on your left.

Alternative route through Wandle Park.

You can go 200 yards further east along High Street, Colliers Wood, to enter Wandle Park (not to be confused with Wandle Park, Croydon) *(toilets). Colliers Wood Station on the Northern Line is 100 yards beyond the park entrance, on the south side of the road. Buses to Wimbledon, Tooting, Wandsworth, Balham.* Wandle Park, part of which is National Trust property, became a public park in 1907.

At the north end of Wandle Bank or Wandle Park you will find the former Merton Flour Mill. This was built by John Rennie in about 1789 and was considered the 'most complete of its kind in England'. It ended its industrial life in the hands of Connolly Leather Ltd, and was converted to flats in 1993/4. A new section of riverside path is planned northwards from here, but at present from Wandle Bank you must turn right past the mill, along Byegrove Road (from the park cross Byegrove Road) to find a footpath leading north at the junction with Denison Road. After 75 yards, go through a wooden gate to your left, then along a rough path across open ground to rejoin the river, which is behind a concrete flood-wall.

Pass underneath the concrete bridge which carries North Road and go into Wandle Meadow Nature Park, formerly a sewage works on the site of water meadows known in the early 16th century as Holmesmead and Bygrave Mead. Continue across the 'meadow' until you get to the railway line. (Shortly before this, a bridge to a recreation ground on the west bank gives a view of the river which is otherwise hidden by concrete walls.) Go through the bridge under the railway line, which is at the right-hand end of the meadow. You then join a raised foot/cycle-path (keep right) known as Mead Path, now diverted from its original line further east. For the first 200 yards, you are beside a subsidiary stream of the River Graveney, which shortly flows into the Wandle.

(8 miles)

The path now follows the main river for 400 yards to reach Plough Lane at Summerstown. *(Refreshments: pubs near Plough Lane/Haydons Road junction.)* Cross Plough Lane with care, go over to the opposite bank of the river, and join a roughly-surfaced riverside path.

Summerstown is first mentioned in 1800, when it was a small hamlet which had probably developed in the late 18th century. The famous Garratt Copper Mills were established there by Dutch Protestant immigrants, where they manufactured brass plates for kettles and skillets, or frying pans, the actual process being kept secret. The works had closed by 1895, although the mill wheel was used by their successor, a leather works, which continued into the 1950s. Silk weaving was a more exotic trade, carried out by one Nicholas Garratt, who made a considerable fortune. On his death, in 1728, he left the Weaver's Company a bequest of East India Stock, valued at £1,700. In the 19th century the Corruganza Box factory took over the premises, which survived until a few years ago. Today, the whole area has been redeveloped, with light industrial units and D-I-Y stores. Little remains now of the old village or the mill buildings. All that survives are some weirs and sluices in the river itself.

Continue northwards along the west bank for about three quarters of a mile, with warehousing and light industry on your left. On your left, at the start of this section, is the former headquarters of Wimbledon Football Club, whose first team now plays at Selhurst Park. About halfway along, on the opposite bank, the main channel of the River Graveney joins the Wandle, though it may be hidden by vegetation. A footbridge is planned to link with Garratt Park here, also on the east bank. The east bank of the next stretch of the Wandle runs by Garratt

20.   The Wandle from the Lydden Road Bridge, Earlsfield, c. 1974. This section has now been improved.

Park. The river bank itself is occupied by allotments. This land used to be part of the Little Garratt Green common land associated with the hamlet of Garratt, which grew up in the 16th century. During the 18th century it was the site of the famous elections of the Mayors of Garratt, a mock political election-cum-carnival. The Leather Bottle public house which dates from this period was the centre of these activities. The west bank is still in the Borough of Merton, and there used to be filter beds for the Wimbledon Sewage Works. These too have now dis-appeared and have been replaced by an industrial estate.

(9 miles)

London Borough of Wandsworth

The final fifty yards of this section of riverside path, leading to the Trewint Street Bridge, is actually in Wandsworth Borough. The Garratt mills once stood at this bridge. These were oil mills, where lin-seed was prepared and crushed to make gallons of linseed oil. The rail-

21. Engineering work at Penwith Road Bridge, Earlsfield in 1958.

way embankment was built for the London and Southampton Railway, which was opened in 1838. The nearby Earlsfield Station, however, did not open until 1884.

There is a proposal to open a new section of riverside path northwards from Trewint Street Bridge - this would save a long and unattractive diversion along the main road. For the present, you must cross the bridge, then turn left along Summerley Street for 250 yards to Garratt Lane *(several pubs and cafes; automatic toilets)*. Turn left *(with Earlsfield railway station opposite)* for 400 yards. The river can be seen from bridges in Penwith and Duntshill Road which both turn off to the left. If you go down these you need to return to Garratt Lane to continue the trail.

During the 19th century there were cloth-printing works at Earlsfield, which in the 1920s were converted into making street lamps. Other

22.   The Wandle at Strathville Road, Wandsworth, in 1958, when the river was at its worst.

industries included a chemical manure factory, another cardboard works, and, on, land between the river and Garratt Lane at the Duntshill bend, a fireworks factory. This consisted of small wooden huts containing the gunpowder work-benches, scattered over an open field. This would have limited any damage caused by an accidental explosion.

At the point where Garratt Lane bears right, go left along St. John's Drive through the Henry Prince Estate, passing through three archways to rejoin the riverside. The Estate was opened in 1938 and named after a local councillor, who actively supported 'decent homes for the working class'.

Go right a little to cross a footbridge over the river into King George's Park *(toilets)*, and then turn right along a riverside path on the west bank for 400 yards. The park was once mainly grazing land, with areas for bleaching cloth. Today, this part of the park is a rather uninteresting flat, open, grass area, mainly laid out as playing fields, but the northern end includes a lake with wildfowl, and a children's zoo.

Continue past the horse-riding centre, and then a children's play-ground, to reach Kimber Road.

(10 miles)

Continue ahead beside the river for 150 yards; then you must divert away from it to continue through the rest of the park, as the way ahead is occupied by an industrial estate.

A short diversion
In another 150 yards, just before the Wandle Recreation Centre (a green and red metal building), you have an opportunity to make a diversion to your right along a brick footpath. This was the site of Henckell's Iron Mill, which produced cast shot, shells and cannon. There were water-powered mechanical hammers and giant shears that could cut through iron bars two inches thick. A book on London, pub-lished in 1792, mentions it as a place to see modern industrial process-es. At the same time there was in existence a paper mill, which import-ed Esparto grass and Tripoli rush from Spain and North Africa. In 1836, the paper mill took over Henckell's premises, and the whole complex became McMurray's Royal Paper Mill. The raw materials were brought up the Thames by barge, and then into a canal that ended in a basin at the rear of the Ram Brewery. The final part of the jour-ney was completed by horse and cart. A light engineering firm, Benham and Sons, took over part of the site in 1913, the rest being occupied by the Veritas Gas Mantle Factory. These in turn have been replaced by the ubiquitous light industrial units.

When you reach Garratt Lane, turn left and go to the Mapleton Road Bridge, a short distance ahead. From here you can look downstream and see the river disappearing beneath the Arndale Centre, a complex of council flats and a shopping centre, completed in 1973. This was the site of the Upper Mill, which can be traced back to the mid-16th century, and probably existed much earlier. For much of its life it was a flour mill, and by the mid-19th century had been acquired by Messrs Watney and Wells, who also owned the Middle Mill and the Lower or

23.   The Wandle from Buckhold Bridge, Wandsworth. This section of the river is
now below the Arndale Centre.

Causeway Mill. Between them they worked 31 pairs of grindstones
and produced 60,000 sacks of flour a year. The importance of the
Wandsworth flour mills was recognised in 1610, when it was largely
due to the opposition of local 'mealmen', that water was not drawn off
from the Wandle to supply the City of London. The Upper Mill was
much altered and added to during the 18th and 19th centuries. In 1926,
one of the main buildings was burnt down, whilst the other major part,
a square, four-floored, weatherboarded building, survived until 1962,
when it was demolished as a dangerous structure.

You then have to go left along Mapleton Road to rejoin the Wandle
Trail route inside the park.

If not making the diversion, continue northwards, passing to the left of
the Wandle Recreation Centre and an open-air swimming-pool, (now
closed) to the park's Mapleton Road entrance. Turn left here, go along
the brick path, and then right, towards the tennis courts *(automatic toilet)* to enter the ornamental section of the park, with the lake. If you
go to the right of the lake, into Neville Gill Close, you will find an

entrance to the Arndale Centre *(refreshments, toilets)*. The Trail follows the left side of the lake to leave the park by the main entrance and exit, at Buckhold Road. Turn right and walk 200 yards to Wandsworth High Street, which you cross at traffic lights *(automatic toilet including disabled)*.

After crossing the High Street, straight ahead from the main entrance of the Arndale Centre, you must turn left (but before doing so go right a few yards to find a small riverside oasis on the site of an old public house called The Bull, which was destroyed by bombing in the Second World War). Young's Brewery is on the opposite bank. There has been a brewery on the site since the 17th century, if not earlier. The Wandle emerges here after passing under the Arndale Centre and the road bridge. The bridge's origins are lost in the mists of time, and may even date from the Roman period. The first recorded evidence is from the minutes of the Surrey and Kent Sewer Commissioners for 1569, when a stone bridge is mentioned at Wandsworth. However, legend has it that in about 1601 it was in such a bad state of repair that Queen Elizabeth I was forced to ford the river and get her feet wet. She issued an order that the bridge was to be repaired forthwith, which was duly done in 1602. This bridge lasted until 1757 when it was widened; and it was widened again in 1820, to take the improved turnpike road. Another widening and strengthening took place in 1912, with yet another rebuild just about to take place.

Return to the road crossing, and, shortly after, turn right along Wandsworth Plain, which contains a fine Queen Anne terrace dated 1723. At the end of the road cross to the left-hand side, and then cross Armoury Way at the traffic lights. Turn right *(passing the Crane pub)*.

At the northern end of the brewery, next to Armoury Way, is the site of the Wandsworth Middle or Brazil Mill. No doubt it started life as a corn mill, but by 1578 it was crushing 'Brassil' wood to produce a scarlet dye, for which Wandsworth became famous, although the business was short-lived, as the mill had returned to corn grinding by 1610.

On the north side of the road, there was once a cattle pound, which was swept away when Armoury Way was put through in 1938, as was an old pub called The Bells.

24.   Cutting osiers (willows) at an unknown Wandleside location, c. 1870-80. This was once an important industry, as the willow was used for basketwork.

Bear left along The Causeway, which is now a quiet, pedestrianised street. There were once two important industries in this area. The first was that of Messrs. Wentworth and Sons, an engineering firm, who principally made beam-engines. Two examples still survive in working order in Young's Brewery, one made in 1835 and the other in 1867. The other firm was Blackmore's Bolting Cloth factory. 'Bolting' cloth was a material that sifted newly-ground flour, dividing it into a fine quality, and a coarse quality with bran. The important point about the cloth was that it was seamless, and so did not become clogged with the residue.

Proceed along the Causeway. After a short distance you come to a sluice between the former pond of Lower Mill on your right, and the tidal Bell Lane Creek on your left. Just beyond this there is a small area of land which is managed as a nature reserve by the London Wildlife Trust.

Pass under the railway bridge, and then cross the main channel on a very narrow footbridge, beyond which is a barrier which cannot be negotiated by wheelchairs (though this point is accessible from Smugglers Way to the east). Here the Wandle-mouth is just visible, with Feathers Wharf on its right - you may need to stand on a nearby low wall to see them.

Originally, the delta was a wild place, dotted with low, ever-changing islands, used only for rough grazing and the growing of osiers. In Tudor times it was said to have been a favourite place for smugglers to bring their contraband ashore. In the second half of the 19th century it was drained and built up with dumped material. It gradually became covered with industrial buildings, including another fireworks factory and a cattle-feed manufactory.

The land immediately to your left is the site of Wandsworth's Lower or Causeway Mill which straddled the Wandle. This was a long, clapper-board-faced structure; and, in the 17th century, wheat was brought from Brentford and Kingston to be ground at this mill. It was demolished at the turn of this century. A spit of land juts northward, separating the mill stream from the Bell Lane Creek branch. This is overgrown, and is a favourite nesting place for herons. Near here stood an old pub and boat house called The Feathers. The name survives in Wandsworth Council's Feathers Wharf, visible to the left, where the local refuse was taken away by barge. This has been replaced by the modern waste transfer station a few yards to the east. This area was once covered by the Wandsworth Gas Works, and after its demolition was left derelict for years. The area is slowly being redeveloped, and any plans will have to include a pedestrian walk along the Wandle and the Thames.

There is a much better view from the west bank, though it requires a substantial diversion: from Armoury Way go north along Frogmore, right along Putney Bridge Road, right along Point Pleasant and Osiers Road, then right along Enterprise Way - here is a short but quite pleasant section of Thames riverside "promenade". A new development is underway (1996) which will open up this part of the river, including the old landing place of Judge's Steps. The early 19th century Prospect House is to be restored and turned into flats.

25.   The Wandle flowing into the Thames at Wandsworth.

(11 miles)

This is the end of the Wandle Trail.   Congratulations if you have walked the whole route, and we hope that you enjoyed it, whatever your distance. *For Wandsworth Town Railway Station, continue east along The Causeway, passing the Western Riverside Waste Transfer Station, then keep ahead along Smugglers Way (shown on older maps as Friendship Way) for 300 yards to the main road (Swandon Way). Cross at the lights, then continue ahead along Old York Road, shortly bearing right to pass under the railway bridge to the station. Refreshments can be obtained at a McDonalds by the junction of Smugglers Way and Swandon Way. The Ship pub beside the Thames is close at hand along Jews Row (behind McDonalds), and there are several pubs and bistros near Wandsworth Town station.*

The Geology of the River

Throughout historic times, the collective source of the River Wandle has been at the foot of the North Downs, in a line of strong springs extending westward from Croydon through Waddon and Wallington to Carshalton. However, it is apparent that the wide and deep spreads of sand and gravel, through which the river then flows northward to the River Thames, are too extensive to have been laid down by the existing small river: an earlier and more effective period of erosion and deposition is indicated.

It is sometimes argued that, many millions of years ago, the Wandle originated in the Weald and flowed northwards across the North Downs through the Merstham gap, where the Croydon to Brighton road now passes over the Downs. According to this 'Wealden Wandle' theory the uppermost stretches of the River Mole should be seen as a survival of the head-waters of the Wandle. Evidence for this theory may be provided by the chert pebbles to be found in the Wandle gravel deposits. These pebbles can also be accounted for by the alternative view that the chert derives from the clay with flint deposits capping the higher points of the Downs themselves, and most geologists believe that the river developed on the chalk.

Terminating about ten thousand years ago, the last Ice Age had been a time of alternating cold and warm periods, during which the periglacial (surrounding the glaciers) area of southern England, south of the ice sheets, was subjected to alternating intensive freezing, and thawing. Where exposed to the elements, chalk is especially vulnerable to the periglacial erosion caused by these repetitive processes. Saturated chalk has a high water content because of its high porosity. Freezing in icy conditions, the contained water expands and breaks down the solid chalk to rubble. Early in the Ice Age the gentle northern slope of the downs had a Tertiary (geologically recent) cover of sands, clays, and pebble beds; less permeable than chalk, and extending far higher than it does today. When stream erosion on the surface of this cover exposed the underlying chalk along the valley floors, persistent freeze-thaw action rapidly deepened the valley bottoms. Spring floods from melting snow carried quantities of chalk debris, with its content of coarse broken flint and Tertiary pebbles, along the narrow channels, further scouring and deepening them. Today the resulting intricate system of deep valleys remains in the downs above Croydon as the branching Caterham and Smitham Bottom Valley network. From it, the great fans of periglacial debris, washed out northward at Croydon on to the lower ground in the Ice Age, have been left as the descending terraces of sand and gravel in the Wandle Valley.

The composition of the Wandle sands and gravels proves their Ice Age origin. Normal river deposits consist, in the main, of rounded pebbles in stratified well-washed silt and sand. By contrast, the Wandle deposits, both along the downland valley floors and in the outwash terraces to the north, largely consist of unsorted, roughly abraded, flint eroded from the chalk, mixed with sand and pre-rounded pebbles derived from the Tertiary cover. Locally, the valley gravels also contain great blocks of conglomerate from the Tertiary Blackheath Beds, too heavy for normal river transport. Falling to the north, the outwash terraces show three main levels: an upper, older, level, in eastern Croydon, known as the Fairfield Terrace; a second, much larger, spread called the Mitcham Terrace, stretching along the Wandle valley from Old Town, Croydon; and a third, much younger, and more restricted, terrace at Wandsworth, grading into the flood plain of the River Thames.

The remains of cold-climate mammals, such as mammoths, are recorded from the Fairfield and Mitcham Terraces, as well as from the downland valley deposits, further proof of their Ice Age origin. Once established, all the terraces would have been subjected to reworking in ensuing Arctic-like periods, often with the addition of later superficial layers. The discovery of peat in silt, with wood fragments and fossil insects, at Beddington, shows that at least the southern upper end of the Mitcham Terrace dates from the closing stages of the Ice Age. The wood gave a radiocarbon date of just over 8000 years BC, a date confirmed by the remains of cold-climate insects, many of which are extinct in Britain today.

With the end of the Ice Age came the cessation of periglacial outwash from the downland valleys, and, as they dried up, the Wandle's source of water slowly shrank to the perennial line of springs along the foot of the downland slope west of Croydon. This is where, at a number of points, water in the saturated chalk, derived from percolating rainwater, escapes over the edge of its cover of impermeable Tertiary clays, collectively to form surface drainage: the River Wandle. Due to variations in rainfall, the level of saturation in the chalk fluctuates, so that throughout historic times, springs have sometimes broken out at higher levels in the dry-valley system, giving rise to temporary bournes. A general lowering of the water table in the chalk has resulted in the gradual decline of these sporadic flows. However, the Caterham and Coulsdon bournes rise occasionally. A thin deposit of river silt, left by the bournes and augmented by hillwash, masks the coarse Ice Age gravels along the valley floors. It also occurs in several small dry valleys above the springs at Carshalton, from which a separate stream flows to join the main river from Croydon.

Archaeology

The earliest remains of human activity which have been found in the Wandle Valley are flint artefacts, including a large collection of Palaeolithic (pre 10,000 BC) flint tools from near St. Anne's Church, Wandsworth.

With the passing of the last Ice Age, came the Mesolithic period, or Middle Stone Age (7,000 - 4,000 B.C.) when people still depended on hunting and fishing, and favoured dry sites close to rivers and lakes for occupation. Numerous characteristic implements from this period have been found around the head-waters of the Wandle at Waddon, Beddington and Carshalton, usually on the dry soils of the Thanet Sand beds overlooking the spring-line. One such site was excavated at Orchard Hill, Carshalton, during 1964-5, where 15,000 pieces of struck flint of Mesolithic and later date were found, along with many fish bones.

During the Neolithic period (4000 - 2000 B.C.) knowledge of agriculture and animal husbandry was introduced to Britain, together with technological innovations such as making pottery and fine-ground and polished stone tools. However, evidence for settlement in this period along the Wandle is sparse. There is no clear break between the Neolithic and the Bronze Age. The archaeological record for the Earlier Bronze Age (c.2300 - 1200 B.C.) is limited, but the recent

(1992) discovery of a smashed collared urn of this period, in the grounds of Carshalton House (now St. Philomena's School), suggests the existence of settlement in this area, very close to a source of the Wandle.

The archaeological record expands extensively in the Later Bronze Age period (c.1200 - 700 B.C.) when a mass of bronze-work was deposited in the Thames close to the mouth of the Wandle. A concentration of bronze hoards of this period has been found in the Carshalton-Beddington-Croydon area; where there is also substantial evidence of settlement, at sites such as the Beddington Sewage Farm; Carshalton House; the former Wandle Valley Hospital site; and the major site at the former Queen Mary's Hospital, Carshalton. The latter is now recognised as an early defended enclosure of the 10th to 8th centuries BC. It is likely that, during this period, when the climate is considered to have been warmer than today, people began to exploit the head-waters of the Wandle more extensively, and no doubt also used the dip-slope of the Downs to the south, for settlement. On most of the above sites, finds continue into the early Iron Age (from c. 700 BC), but there is a marked decrease in the amount of material for the Iron Age in general, although the Thames was the recipient of much metalwork; probably votive offerings, such as the famous Battersea shield, now in the British Museum.

Roman rule brought new improved technology to Britain, and an increase in the production of materials like pottery and tile, which tend to survive as archaeological finds. Villas, farmhouses, and other rural buildings were more substantially built, and their remains frequently survive. To date, the only recorded Roman villa near the Wandle was on the site of Beddington Sewage Farm, where the remains of the house, bath-house, a succession of large barns and other buildings, and a well, were excavated in the early 1980s.

Another major feature of Roman occupation was the road network. Stane Street, which ran from London to Chichester, crossed the Wandle near Merton Bridge, and there is some evidence of settlement close to it. Another Roman road passed through Croydon, where there is also evidence for settlement. Recent excavations uncovered Roman remains near the Coombe Hill Water Tower, and in the dry valley which is now occupied by South Croydon. Small quantities of Romano-British material are spread throughout the Wandle Valley along the river's course, and cemeteries from this period have been found at Beddington, Mitcham and Wandsworth.

After the withdrawal of the Roman administration, and the subsequent immigration by Germanic peoples usually referred to as Anglo-Saxons, history becomes hazier, and archaeology and philology - the study of place-names - assume greater importance. In the Wandle valley the period is represented by early Saxon cemeteries at Croydon, Beddington and Mitcham. Wallington means 'Welsh tun', a settlement of the Celtic, or Romano-British peoples, presumably surrounded by Saxons. The 'Merebank' is a straight ridge, now forming the Beddington/Croydon parish boundary, but may reflect the territorial divisions of this period. After the area had been converted to Christianity, Croydon became an important ecclesiastical settlement - perhaps in the late-7th or 8th centuries - whilst, to the west, Wallington was a royal manor which gave its name to the local Hundred, a Saxon administrative unit. None of the parish churches along the Wandle valley has definite Saxon fabric, but some have wall fragments which could predate the Norman Conquest; and, in the Domesday survey of 1086, churches are recorded at Croydon, Beddington, Carshalton, Merton, and Wimbledon. These churches were associated with settlements which have persisted to the present day.

Ecclesiastical establishments

By 1086 Croydon belonged to the Archbishop of Canterbury; and, in the Middle Ages, it became the location of a major ecclesiastical palace, and parts of the building, including the Great Hall, survive. Henry VIII stayed there, but complained that it was so near the water that he was always ill. In the 18th century it was turned into a wash-house for a textile bleaching ground, and is now a school, although that use is now ceasing, and it may become more accessible to the public as an historic building.

Merton Priory (1117-1538), which was extensively excavated by the Museum of London between 1986 and 1991, occupied some sixty acres south of Merton High Street, on what is now the site of the

Merton Abbey Mills car-park. Fragments of the precinct walls, a rebuilt doorway from the Guest House and the foundations of the Chapter House can still be seen. After demolition to provide stone for Henry VIII's Nonsuch Palace, the land was sold: but the priory's mills continued to function in lay hands, and the Gate-house, and what may have been the Guest House, became private residences. Over a century later, the remainder of the priory site was being used as bleaching grounds.

Historic Houses

An important aspect of the history of the Wandle is the story of its great houses, and even today it is possible to traverse much of the length of the river above Wimbledon as a series of steps from one estate to another. In many larger properties the Wandle was used as an ornamental feature. Relatively few of these estates retain anything approaching their country-house character. Quite a number, including Waddon Court, Carew Manor, The Grange, The Grove, Carshalton Park, Ravensbury Manor, and Morden Hall, have left us their parks; even if little trace of the succession of manor houses which once stood in them remains. One or two have the old parish church adjacent to them, marking their former status. The most complete example is Carew Manor, Beddington, with its medieval Great Hall embedded in a complex mass of post-medieval building, and flanked by the late medieval and Victorian church of St Mary. In the late Middle Ages these estates had largely been owned by members of the aristocracy and important government officials, who found it convenient to have a rural retreat close to London; but by the 17th and 18th centuries, they had for the most part become the preserve of prosperous City businessmen, merchants, and lawyers, or senior army and navy officers, who relished the prospect of a double life as country squires.

Carshalton was particularly rich in this type of property. Carshalton House (c.1700) is still surrounded by a complete informal landscape garden of the late 18th century, while, to the south-east, Carshalton Park is a mere rump surviving from a much larger 130-acre park; the house has also gone, but the building believed to have been the orangery remains, as does the famous grotto, which was itself a celebrated source of the Wandle. A fine Queen Anne house, known as the

26. The ponds at Carshalton in 1896. The building to the right is Honeywood, which is without the Edwardian extension, added in 1903. The Greyhound is on the left.

Old Rectory, still stands near Carshalton ponds. Honeywood, which faces eastward across the ponds, also dates from the late 17th century. It was greatly extended and updated in the late 19th and early 20th centuries when it belonged to John Pattinson Kirk, a merchant. It is now Sutton's Heritage Centre, and includes a room devoted to the Wandle. A little downstream from the ponds is Stone Court, where 18th and 19th buildings stand on or close to the site of the medieval sub-manor of Stone Court. Further downstream Strawberry Lodge still stands in Mill Lane, immediately west of the river. The building appears to have been erected for the gunpowder maker, Josiah Deweye, towards the end of the 17th century. Below this The Culvers stood on a large island in the river. It was built around 1840 for the Quaker banker Samuel Gurney and was one of a number of pleasant country houses of assorted sizes that stood along this stretch of the river. Most appear to have dated from the 19th century, but some, such as the Limes, had a longer but little-known history.

A surviving Wandle house is Bishopsford, which stands above the west side of the river just above Mitcham Bridge. The core of the house is in Gothic style and dates from the mid-19th century.

Downstream from the bridge, Mitcham Grove was one of the most beautifully situated properties on the river, briefly in the ownership of Lord Clive of India, and then the property of the banker Henry Hoare. Part of the grounds survive, but in the main they are covered by a housing estate. Further on, Morden Hall in Morden Hall Park, appears to date from 1750. The site of its Tudor predecessor, Growtes or Growte House is nearby. This was built in 1553 for Edward Whitchurch who, with Richard Grafton, published Miles Coverdale's English Bible, a copy of which, under Henry VIII's legislation, had to be placed in all parish churches. After the Roman Catholic Queen Mary came to the throne in 1554, Whitchurch considered it prudent to leave the country, and he sold the house to a Richard Garth.

Further downstream was a house called Merton Place, which was purchased by Lord Nelson in 1801 on the advice of Lady Hamilton. Water was drawn from the Wandle to form streams and ponds in the garden, and nicknamed 'The Nile' after the river where Nelson won a famous naval victory.

27.   The Culvers house, which stood just south of Culvers Avenue, was erected for the Quaker banker Samuel Gurney, in the 1840s.

Wandle Park, just north of Merton High Street, preserves the location of Wandle Bank House, whose owner, James Perry, a friend of Nelson, also owned the nearby mill. Most of the proprietors of these estates had no objection to taking a share in the profits which the riverside industries could also offer them, and the history of their houses should not be separated from them.

As the topographical artist, Hassell so aptly wrote in 1817, the Wandle was seen to possess many charms; "it can boast of giving a splendour to trade and a repose from its fatigues; every quarter of a mile its course is accompanied by elegant chateaux, and obstructed by commerce - mills succeed each other at short distances down the stream".

In 1889 a writer found that the upper Wandle had become the "pet of the wealthy" because "no longer does it flood its watercress beds and turn vulgar mill wheels, but now winds through lovely gardens where money and ingenuity are devoted to developing its beauties, where bowers and charming vistas, rustic bridges, glens, glades and varied vegetation form a fit setting for its crystal loveliness".

28. Merton Place, once the home of Lord Nelson.

Industrial History

The fast-flowing waters of the Wandle, with a markedly higher average fall per mile in its upper reaches, made the river useless for navigation but ideal for mills. The water-powered corn mill dates back to the Roman empire; the Domesday Book records at least thirteen of these mills on the Wandle - more than half of them above Mitcham - and it is almost certain that downland parishes like Woodmansterne and Banstead also had their mills in the river valley. By 1610 there were no less than 24 corn mills on the Wandle, and at both ends of it one can find mill sites where corn has been ground more or less continuously from the Norman Conquest to the late 19th or early 20th century, as at Waddon and Carshalton and the immense flour mills of Wandsworth, the lowest of which was a tide mill.

At least one fulling mill operated on the river in the Middle Ages. This was used for beating cloth with water-powered hammers to clean, thicken and felt it. A site in Carshalton was being used for grinding dyewood in the second half of the 16th century; but the major expansion and diversification of mill types occurred in the 17th and 18th centuries. The Shepley Mills at Hackbridge seem to have made a progression from corn to fulling to dyewood, and eventually became a spread of three gunpowder mills, in the mid-17th century, which were afterwards used for copper, oil and leather production. Similarly the Amery Mills at Merton Priory began as monastic corn mills and changed through dyewood and copper to a huge paperboard mill which ceased production in 1984, whilst the Wallington Bridge Mill also ran the gamut from corn to fulling of cloth, then to paper, and finally ended its life as a chocolate factory. The major expansion of the Wandle industries in the early modern period owed much to the expertise of refugees from the Continent, especially those from the Low Countries. They were mainly responsible for the development of the iron-mills at Wandsworth and the copper industry at Carshalton, Merton, Mitcham and Wimbledon.

Wars also left their mark on the Wandle industries. Gunpowder was made at Carshalton and Earlsfield; cannon were bored, during the Napoleonic wars, at Wandsworth and Grove Mill, Butter Hill, Carshalton; jerkins for British troops in the Crimea were manufactured at Mitcham, and many of the numerous leather mills made army boots.

29.   The Pontifex Copper Mill, below Plough Lane Bridge, South Wimbledon, in the early 19th century.

Other industries likely to cause offence by reason of smell or explosion soon followed: Mitcham became a major centre for the making of paints and varnishes, oilcloths and fireworks. Snuff mills, in which dried tobacco was ground to a fine powder, appear around the middle of the 18th century at Beddington, Carshalton, Mitcham and Morden, and, later, at Hackbridge. By this time the Wandle mills had proliferated, or had been adapted to a still greater variety of uses, including the processing of leather, grinding of oil seed, and the processing of felt and fibre. There was a paper mill at Mitcham around 1800, and another at Middle Mill in Carshalton, and Wallington Bridge Mill was also used for this purpose at intervals in the 19th century. Since the mill-owners were particularly concerned about the need to transport their produce to London for sale, they supported both the scheme for a Grand Surrey Canal (proposed in 1795 but never built) and the first public railway actually built in England. This was the Surrey Iron Railway, which ran from Wandsworth to Croydon, from which it continued southwards to Merstham as the Croydon, Merstham and Godstone Railway. There was a spur from Mitcham to the mills at Hackbridge. It operated between 1803 and 1846, when the present railway network began to be laid out. In 1805 James Malcolm speculated about the Wandle "for its length and size, perhaps no river in the

30.   The terminus of the Surrey Iron Railway at Wandsworth Basin in the early 19th century.

world does at this time furnish so many valuable and various manu-factories...".

Not all Wandle-side industries depended on water power. From the 17th century calico bleaching was of importance. The cloth was soaked in various weak chemicals of natural origin, and was then stretched out in the open air to be bleached by the sun. It needed to be moistened at intervals, so water was brought to the sites in shallow water-courses, or trenches. The pure water of the Wandle was also needed for washing-out the chemicals at the end of the process. The craft probably owed much to Low Country and French immigrants, with Dutch bleachers settling in Mitcham as early as the late 16th cen-tury. The development of powerful chemical bleaches in the early 19th century caused the industry to go into rapid decline, and the major bleaching ground at Culvers was sold to make a house and garden.

Huguenot entrepreneurs were prominent in the printing of calico and other fabrics, which developed extensively along the river after 1700, when almost the entire working population of Merton, and three-quarters of Wandsworth, were engaged in the trade. For printing the cloth, Francis Nixon's technique of using copper plates was pioneered in the mid-18th century at Phipps Bridge, in conjunction with the Carshalton partnership of Sir George Amyand and John Anthony Rucker; whilst at the end of the century the beauty of the designs of William Kilburn made his calico bleaching and printing firm at Wallington world-famous. Subsequently the Abbey grounds at Merton came to include two famous printing works, those of William Morris and also those of Arthur Liberty, of which some workshop buildings survive, restored, at 'Abbey Mills'.

The brewing industry also made use good use of the fine quality Wandle water both for the beer itself and for cooling and washing; although later, artesian wells were sunk to provide water. Breweries are recorded in some numbers at both ends of the river by the 18th century. Croydon produced a series of distinguished names, such as Crowleys; Nalder and Collyer; Page and Overton; and, at Wandsworth, Watney had extensive breweries; and the town can still boast Young's Ram Brewery, occupying a site used for this purpose as early as 1675.

The variety of mills operating in the middle of the nineteenth century gives a false impression of continuing prosperity. The Wandle milling industries, their power limited by the flow in the river, and faced with the spread and increasing efficiency of the steam engine, were on the verge of collapse, and their decline in the second half of the century was rapid.

Modern factories, notably those manufacturing chemicals, paints, plastics and electrical components, took over this valuable industrial land and, together with suburban housing estates, covered up many of the mill sites. But there is still much to be seen by those who are prepared to go and look for it, although it is unfortunate that very few water-wheels survive. There are none left in the Boroughs of Croydon and Wandsworth, and only one, at Upper Mill, in The Grove Park, Carshalton; and part of another in the Water Tower in the grounds of Carshalton House (St. Philomena's) survive, out of some 15 recorded

31.   The wheel at Liberty's Mill, Merton, in 1976. This is now incorporated in the Merton Abbey Mills Craft Village.

sites in Sutton.   Only the Borough of Merton is better provided for, with four wheels: two at Ravensbury and one at Morden Hall, both sites having been snuff mills; and one wheel at the Liberty site (Abbey Mills) in Merton itself, the only example currently turning.   During the power shortages after the Second World War the Ravensbury Mill wheels were used to generate electricity during power cuts.

Watercress was formerly grown in shallow beds which were supplied with running water from the river, or from springs and boreholes. The commercial growing of cress started in the early 19th century and the first beds in the Wandle Valley probably date from about 1850.   The operator of a cress bed would raise the water level by about four inches, to flood the plants temporarily, and protect them from frost.   This would encourage early growth and mean that cress was available for most of the year.   Before refrigeration and modern transport it would be one of the few salad stuffs available for this length of time.   The number of beds increased rapidly around the turn of the century, and production appears to have reached a peak in the early 1930s. The industry declined very rapidly after 1937 when it was wrongly blamed for a typhoid outbreak in Croydon, which, after the damage had been done, turned out to be from a polluted well in Addington. The decline increased because land could more profitably be used for building, and because cress became less popular, as a greater variety of fresh vegetables became available through improvements in transport and refrigeration.

Natural History

Despite its being now a truly London river, the nature conservationist can find a wealth of plant and animal life throughout the length of the Wandle. Traditionally it was a rich source of watercress, and, at Carshalton, a twelfth-century version of the village name - Kersalton (probably = Cress Alton) - may suggest that the plant was already common in the river at that time. Wild watercress plants are still to be seen in a number of localities in the upper reaches.

The fast-flowing water from Croydon and Carshalton, as it passes both mill sites and parkland on its route to the Thames, has large, streaming, patches of starwort, pondweeds, unbranched bur reed, and the uncommon stream water crowfoot, in a variety of rich greens, with duckweed and water fern trapped in sheltered corners.

The Wandle's former industrial importance as a source of power ensured that it stayed open, instead of being piped underground like many other Thames tributaries; but this use has also resulted in the present state of the banks. The building of weirs, and partial canalisation with concrete, steel piling, or high timber sides to the river, mean that its full wildlife potential is not realised. Only in places where the banks are low and graded can any marginal vegetation flourish; such as in Beddington Park, at Wilderness Island, The Watermeads, and in Morden Hall Park, where sedges, water plantain, fool's watercress,

32 & 33. (see pictures opposite)   Old and new riverbanks, looking upstream and downstream from the footbridge at Richmond green, Beddington. In the past, much of the river was given wooden or concrete banks, which do not provide a good habitat for wildlife. When the opportunity arises, these are being altered to a more natural form.

reedmace and reed sweetgrass, often shaded by willows, provide an attractive wetland habitat.

The plants control the animals that live in the ecosystem by affording them both food and shelter, and there is sufficient plant life in the river to support many fish. Three-spined stickleback are abundant in some areas. In the past, the Wandle had a fine reputation as a trout stream, and in 1817 it was said that the privately-owned stretches of the Wandle provided as good angling as anywhere in the country. The trout at Carshalton "with marble spots like a tortoise" were famous for their excellence. Huge catches are recorded in the 18th and 19th century accounts, and a good example of a rainbow trout caught at Hackbridge in about 1895 can be seen in Honeywood, the Heritage Centre by Carshalton Ponds. In the middle of the 19th century there were increasing complaints about worsening river conditions, and the last Carshalton trout recorded was around 1915, although some later sightings are claimed, and there have been recent reintroductions.

Rod-fishing for coarse fish declined in the mid-1930s. After that time, the fisheries were perceived to be non-existent for much of the river below Beddington; but, from the late 1960s, the then Greater London Council tackled the problem of pollution, together with the relevant London Boroughs, with some success. The first fish population survey conducted by Thames Water Authority took place in 1978, when sites were investigated between Morden Hall Park and Carshalton. Very poor fisheries were seen throughout, with only sticklebacks being common. Water quality and biological information indicated that some reaches were capable of supporting better fish populations; and a major restocking programme, including various species of freshwater fish and brown trout, was recommended and initiated.

By the time that the National Rivers Authority surveyed the river, the fish populations below Colliers Wood were substantially improved, and casual angling began to occur again in the lower reaches. Modest populations of trout, chub, dace and roach were captured in the upper reaches above Hackbridge, and in the Carshalton branch.

The most recently published fish survey was carried out in 1994. Only sticklebacks were found in the Beddington reaches. Dace, roach, perch and stone loach were caught in the upper reaches between

34. Swans and cygnets at The Grove, Carshalton in 1954.

Hackbridge and Butter Hill, as well as below Goat Bridge. The largest fish populations were downstream from North Road, SW19, where good quantities of eels were caught, as well as in King George's Park, Wandsworth. Dace and roach were probably breeding downstream along the Wandsworth reaches of the river. The disastrous pollution incident at the end of October 1995, has had very adverse effects on the fish population downstream from the effluent entry near Goat Bridge, although restocking is now taking place.

A variety of water invertebrates and molluscs, such as shrimps, water mites, water louse and pond snails, are found in the river. Where children from the nature centre in Morden Hall Park dip their nets, large, freshwater shrimps are frequently in their catch. In appropriate habitats, amphibians are seen, such as the smooth newts in the water channels in the Wandle Valley Nature Park, in Merton.

In turn, both plants and animals support aquatic birds. Mallard, moorhen and coot occur in good numbers along stretches where the habitat is appropriate, especially at Waddon Ponds, Carshalton Ponds, The Watermeads and Morden Hall Park. Moorhen and coot have both increased dramatically in numbers in the last ten years, which is probably due to the more sympathetic management of the river. In many places concrete and timber banks have been removed and replaced by a more 'natural' vegetation-covered earth slope.

Canada geese and tufted duck have both colonised the river in the last decade and now breed each year. In 1992, five broods of tufted duck could be seen on Carshalton Ponds. Herons are a common bird along the river: they can even be seen fishing at night using the street lights. They are increasing in numbers nationally, and are a much more common sight these days. Of particular interest is a roost of up to twenty birds at the confluence of the Wandle and the Thames.

Other birds using the Wandle-mouth include a pair of kingfishers, grey wagtails, great crested grebe, little grebe, cormorants, mallard, coot, moorhen, sandpipers and swans. The latter often breed at Carshalton Ponds and have bred elsewhere. The blue flash of a kingfisher flying away is now a common sight, especially in the winter months. Up to three pairs may breed, and the storm of 1987 has helped them by providing nesting sites in the boles of uprooted trees.

Another characteristic bird of rivers, the grey wagtail, can be found breeding at many of the weirs along the river, which mimic its more usual habitat of fast-flowing upland streams. Lately they have been much in evidence around Honeywood and Carshalton Ponds. On the quieter sections, rarer birds have tried to breed, including teal, water rail, and shelduck: the latter succeeded in raising a brood of nine young in 1993. Sedge warblers and reed warblers can often be heard singing from dense vegetation, and occasionally breed.

Typical suburban species of birds are frequent, such as thrushes, starlings, tits and finches. All three species of woodpecker can be seen, and the lesser spotted woodpecker is common. It is the smallest and most elusive of the woodpeckers, and is often first detected by its drumming. In the wilder parts of the river, blackcap, chiffchaff and whitethroat all breed; with other summer visitors often seen passing through on their migration, including willow warbler, sedge warbler, and, very occasionally, wood warbler.

In winter, the river can be very exciting for bird watchers, particularly after hard spells. In February 1991, when nearly a foot of snow lay on the ground, many birds took refuge along the river where food was still accessible. Several species of rare ducks - smew, goldeneye, scaup and pintail - could be seen. Over a hundred snipe were feeding along the banks, and other wading birds seen were ruff, redshank and green sandpiper. The very cold spell in 1963 resulted in a similar influx, when Slavonian grebe and scaup were seen on the river at Carshalton. In milder winters, siskins and redpolls can sometimes be seen feeding in the alders along the river. Chiffchaff and blackcap are principally summer migrants, but both species overwinter in small numbers and can be seen.

Special mention should be made of Beddington Sewage Farm at Hackbridge, which, because of its undisturbed nature, is one of the best bird-watching areas in London. A channel from the Wandle has been built to a flood alleviation lake, which has added to the diversity of the site, attracting many species of wildfowl, waders and terns. It is for tree sparrows that the farm is most important, having the largest colony in the country. In 1992, one hundred nest boxes were erected, and, each year, about fifty boxes are used, and another thirty pairs use other nesting holes. The site has been the subject of a planning application for gravel extraction, with restoration by landfill and habitat creation, which was granted after a public inquiry in 1995.

The Wandle flows through a succession of notable parks, and many fine specimens of trees can be seen among the extensive meadowlands conserved in this way. In such situations their branches can spread out to their full extent, unhampered by the restricting competition they would encounter in woodland habitats. As would be expected along river banks, native willows are plentiful. So are poplars. There are magnificent plane trees in Ravensbury Park; and a huge plane tree, once thought to be the largest in the country, stands near the Upper Pond at Carshalton. Large limes and horse chestnuts are a particular feature of Beddington Park. The Grange has two old mulberries, a Caucasian wingnut, and Wellingtonias, amongst other specimen trees.

The planting of shrubs and trees, both native and non-native species, is valuable for wildlife. The path between Windsor Avenue and the Savacentre, in Merton, is notable for its sheltered environment; and, on a sunny day in summer, butterflies can always be seen here. Fences are found covered with trailing plants including hops - are they remnants of earlier hop fields in the vicinity? Parts of the river banks provide cover for foxes, other small mammals, and even rabbits. Bats are frequently seen along the Carshalton Park water-courses, and in Beddington Park.

Wetlands are the home of a number of insects. Alongside the river, where the high banks preclude wetland species, there is often a diversity of nutrient-enriched and disturbed-soil vegetation, including nettles, docks, mugwort, Japanese knotweed, and garden escapees, such as Michaelmas daisies, all of which provide the right conditions for many insects and their larvae, including butterflies and moths. At Spencer Road Wetlands, Hackbridge, several species of rare moths are found in the reedbed which has developed in an old watercress bed.

Dragonflies and damselflies are more characteristic of rivers of the open countryside, but several species do occur on the Wandle. The commonest is the blue-tailed damselfly, which readily tolerates more polluted waters. In 1994, it could be seen along the riverbank at Earlsfield, and by the unofficial nature reserve at The Causeway, Wandsworth. The banded demoiselle is a particularly attractive species, its slow dancing flight showing off the blue bands on the wings. It can be seen above The Watermeads, and has even been seen in Colliers Wood High Street.

Ten years ago, apart from The Watermeads, there were no nature reserves along the river; now it is almost impossible to keep track of them all. Wilderness Island and Spencer Road Wetlands, both managed by London Wildlife Trust, are two of the oldest. Bennett's Hole, near The Watermeads, is more recent. Volunteers have worked on many other sections of the river to create more attractive habitats for wildlife. There are examples in Dale Park, near the old site of Wandle Valley Hospital, and Morden Hall Park.

In 1992, The Wandle Valley Nature Park was opened on the site of the former sewage works at North Road, alongside the river, but divided from it by a large concrete wall. A diversity of habitats, including ponds, has been created there, partly using former structures. The area of untamed vegetation between Plough Lane, Wimbledon, and Trewint

35.   Volunteers working on a new wildlife pond on the site of the former Wandle
Valley Hospital, 1986.

36.   The Wandle at Spencer Road, Hackbridge. This is one of the few sections of
the river which has a natural appearance.

Street, Earlsfield, is about to be developed as a further nature reserve.
There are also two nature reserves at the Wandle-mouth, one on The
Spit, and the other (unofficial) at the Causeway, on electricity compa-
ny land.

Two valuable nature education centres have been developed in recent
years along the river, one in the old Snuff Mill in Morden Hall Park, and
the other in the Ecology Centre near Carshalton Ponds. Plenty of survey
work in a number of environmental fields is being done, and much is
being done by enthusiastic volunteers from each borough along the river.

Selective Bibliography

There is a very substantial literature on the Wandle and on the history of the towns and villages along it. The following bibliography concentrates on the river, with an emphasis on more modern works.

General
Batley, J. The Bourne through the ages. *Bourne Society Local History Records,* i, 1962.
Bayliss, D.A. *Retracing the First Public Railway.* 2nd edition, 1985.
Braithwaite, F. On the Rise and Fall of the River Wandle. *Proceedings of the Institution of Civil Engineers,* xx, 1860-61; pp.191-258.
Hillier, J. *Old Surrey Watermills,* 1951.
Giuseppi, M.S. The River Wandle in 1610. *Surrey Archaeological Collections,* xxi, 1908; pp.170-191.
Hassell, J. *Picturesque rides and walks within thirty miles of the British Metropolis,* 1817-18.
Hobson, J.M. *The Book of the Wandle,* 1924.
Latham, B. Croydon Bourne Flows. *Proceedings of the C.N.H.S.S.,* vi, 1904.
Latham, B. Records of Underground Water and the Croydon Bourne Flows. *Proceedings of the C.N.H.S.S,* viii, 1917; pp.113-125.
Malcolm, J. *A Compendium of Modern Husbandry principally written during a survey of Surrey,* 1805.
Newbury, K.M. The Bourne Through the Ages. *Bourne Society Local History Records,* xiii, 1974.
Wandle Group. *The River Wandle: A guide and handbook,* 1974.

Geology and Environment
National Rivers Authority. *The Wandle, Beverley Brook, Hogsmill Catchment Management plan: Action plan.* July 1995.
Peake, D.S. The Age of the Wandle Gravels in the Vicinity of Croydon. *Proceedings of the C.N.H.S.S.,* xiv, 1971; pp.145-161.
Whitaker, W. The Water Supply of Surrey. *Memoirs of the Geological Survey,* 1912.
Yarham, I., Barnes, R. and Britton, B. *Nature conservation in Sutton.* London Ecology Unit, 1993.

Croydon
Anderson, J. *Chronicles of Croydon,* 1864-1879.

Gent, J. *Croydon: The Story of a Hundred Years.* C.N.H.S.S., 5th edition, 1979.

Sutton

Jones, A.E. *An Illustrated Directory of Old Carshalton.* 1973.
Jones, A.E. *The Story of Carshalton House.* Sutton Libraries & Arts Services, 1980.
Phillips, J. *A Short Guide to Carew Manor.* Sutton Leisure Services, 1989.
Smee, A. *My Garden: Its Plan and Culture.* 1872.

Merton

Bruce, P. and Mason, S. *Merton Priory.* 1993.
Jowett, E.M. *An Illustrated History of Merton and Morden.* 1951.
Montague, E.N. *Textile Bleaching and Printing in Mitcham and Merton 1590-1870.* 1992.
Prentis, W.H. *Snuff Mill Story.* 1970.
Wandle Industrial Museum. *An Hour Passed at Merton Abbey.* 1987 (Part of a series in progress).

Wandsworth

Green, G.W.C. *The Story of Wandsworth and Putney.* c.1925/6.